T. S. Eliot

The Waste Land
and Other Poems

T. S. (Thomas Stearns) Eliot (1888–1965) was born and raised in St. Louis, Missouri, and spent many of his adult years in England. He worked for a bank while writing poetry, teaching, and reviewing, and was recognized as a major force in the literary world with his publication of *The Waste Land* in 1922.

The Waste Land
and Other Poems

The Waste Land
and Other Poems

T. S. Eliot

VINTAGE CLASSICS
Vintage Books
A Division of Penguin Random House LLC
New York

FIRST VINTAGE CLASSICS EDITION, MAY 2021

Published in the United States by Vintage Books,
a division of Penguin Random House LLC, New York, and
distributed in Canada by Penguin
Random House Canada Limited, Toronto.

Vintage is a registered trademark and Vintage Classics and
colophon are trademarks of Penguin Random House LLC.

**Vintage Classics Trade Paperback
ISBN: 978-0-593-31334-3
eBook ISBN: 978-0-593-31335-0**

Book design by Steven E. Walker

www.vintagebooks.com

Printed in the United States of America
8th Printing

CONTENTS

THE WASTE LAND (1922)

THE HOLLOW MEN (1925)

The Waste Land
and Other Poems

PRUFROCK AND OTHER OBSERVATIONS
1917

For Jean Verdenal, 1889–1915
mort aux Dardanelles

Or puoi la quantitate
comprender dell'amor ch'a te mi scalda,
quando dismento nostra vanitate,
trattando l'ombre come cosa salda.

THE LOVE SONG OF J. ALFRED PRUFROCK

S'io credessi che mia risposta fosse
a persona che mai tornasse al mondo,
questa fiamma staria senza più scosse.
Ma perciocchè che giammai di questo fondo
non tornò vivo alcun, s'i'odo il vero,
senza tema d'infamia ti rispondo.

Let us go then, you and I,
When the evening is spread out against the sky
Like a patient etherised upon a table;
Let us go, through certain half-deserted streets,
5   The muttering retreats
Of restless nights in one-night cheap hotels
And sawdust restaurants with oyster-shells:
Streets that follow like a tedious argument
Of insidious intent
10 To lead you to an overwhelming question . . .
Oh, do not ask, "What is it?"
Let us go and make our visit.

In the room the women come and go
Talking of Michelangelo.

15 The yellow fog that rubs its back upon the window-panes,
The yellow smoke that rubs its muzzle on the window-
    panes,
Licked its tongue into the corners of the evening,
Lingered upon the pools that stand in drains,

Let fall upon its back the soot that falls from chimneys,
20 Slipped by the terrace, made a sudden leap,
And seeing that it was a soft October night,
Curled once about the house, and fell asleep.

And indeed there will be time
For the yellow smoke that slides along the street
25 Rubbing its back upon the window-panes;
There will be time, there will be time
To prepare a face to meet the faces that you meet;
There will be time to murder and create,
And time for all the works and days of hands
30 That lift and drop a question on your plate;
Time for you and time for me,
And time yet for a hundred indecisions,
And for a hundred visions and revisions,
Before the taking of a toast and tea.

35 In the room the women come and go
Talking of Michelangelo.

And indeed there will be time
To wonder, "Do I dare?" and, "Do I dare?"
Time to turn back and descend the stair,
40 With a bald spot in the middle of my hair—
(They will say: "How his hair is growing thin!")
My morning coat, my collar mounting firmly to the chin,
My necktie rich and modest, but asserted by a simple pin—
(They will say: "But how his arms and legs are thin!")
45 Do I dare

Disturb the universe?
In a minute there is time
For decisions and revisions which a minute will reverse.

For I have known them all already, known them all—
50   Have known the evenings, mornings, afternoons,
I have measured out my life with coffee spoons;
I know the voices dying with a dying fall
Beneath the music from a farther room.
     So how should I presume?

55   And I have known the eyes already, known them all—
The eyes that fix you in a formulated phrase,
And when I am formulated, sprawling on a pin,
When I am pinned and wriggling on the wall,
Then how should I begin
60   To spit out all the butt-ends of my days and ways?
     And how should I presume?
And I have known the arms already, known them all—
Arms that are braceleted and white and bare
(But in the lamplight, downed with light brown hair!)
65   Is it perfume from a dress
That makes me so digress?
Arms that lie along a table, or wrap about a shawl.
     And should I then presume?
     And how should I begin?

                    * * * *

70   Shall I say, I have gone at dusk through narrow streets
And watched the smoke that rises from the pipes

Of lonely men in shirt-sleeves, leaning out of windows? . . .
   I should have been a pair of ragged claws
Scuttling across the floors of silent seas.

* * * *

75 And the afternoon, the evening, sleeps so peacefully!
   Smoothed by long fingers,
   Asleep . . . tired . . . or it malingers,
   Stretched on the floor, here beside you and me.
   Should I, after tea and cakes and ices,
80 Have the strength to force the moment to its crisis?
   But though I have wept and fasted, wept and prayed,
   Though I have seen my head (grown slightly bald) brought
     in upon a platter,
   I am no prophet—and here's no great matter;
   I have seen the moment of my greatness flicker,
   And I have seen the eternal Footman hold my coat,
85   and snicker,
   And in short, I was afraid.

   And would it have been worth it, after all,
   After the cups, the marmalade, the tea,
   Among the porcelain, among some talk of you and me,
90 Would it have been worth while,
   To have bitten off the matter with a smile,
   To have squeezed the universe into a ball
   To roll it towards some overwhelming question,
   To say: "I am Lazarus, come from the dead,
95 Come back to tell you all, I shall tell you all"—
   If one, settling a pillow by her head,

Should say: "That is not what I meant at all.
That is not it, at all."

And would it have been worth it, after all,
100   Would it have been worth while,
After the sunsets and the dooryards and the sprinkled streets,
After the novels, after the teacups, after the skirts that trail
       along the floor—
And this, and so much more?—
It is impossible to say just what I mean!
105   But as if a magic lantern threw the nerves in patterns on a
       screen:
Would it have been worth while
If one, settling a pillow by her head,
Should say, "That is not what I meant at all;
       "That is not it, at all."

* * * *

110   No! I am not Prince Hamlet, nor was meant to be;
Am an attendant lord, one that will do
To swell a progress, start a scene or two,
Advise the prince; no doubt, an easy tool,
Deferential, glad to be of use,
115   Politic, cautious, and meticulous;
Full of high sentence, but a bit obtuse;
At times, indeed, almost ridiculous—
Almost, at times, the Fool.

I grow old . . . I grow old . . .
120   I shall wear the bottoms of my trousers rolled.

Shall I part my hair behind? Do I dare to eat a peach?
I shall wear white flannel trousers, and walk upon the
    beach.
I have heard the mermaids singing, each to each.
I do not think that they will sing to me.

125   I have seen them riding seaward on the waves
Combing the white hair of the waves blown back
When the wind blows the water white and black.

We have lingered in the chambers of the sea
By sea-girls wreathed with seaweed red and brown
130   Till human voices wake us, and we drown.

PORTRAIT OF A LADY

Thou hast committed—
Fornication: but that was in another country,
And besides, the wench is dead.
                    —The Jew of Malta

I

    Among the smoke and fog of a December afternoon
You have the scene arrange itself—as it will seem to do—
With "I have saved this afternoon for you";
And four wax candles in the darkened room,
5   Four rings of light upon the ceiling overhead,
An atmosphere of Juliet's tomb
Prepared for all the things to be said, or left unsaid.
We have been, let us say, to hear the latest Pole
Transmit the Preludes, through his hair and finger-tips.
10 "So intimate, this Chopin, that I think his soul
Should be resurrected only among friends
Some two or three, who will not touch the bloom
That is rubbed and questioned in the concert room."
—And so the conversation slips
15 Among velleities and carefully caught regrets
Through attenuated tones of violins
Mingled with remote cornets
And begins.
"You do not know how much they mean to me, my
    friends,
20 And how, how rare and strange it is, to find
In a life composed so much, so much of odds and ends,

(For indeed I do not love it . . . you knew? you are not
     blind!
How keen you are!)
To find a friend who has these qualities,
25   Who has, and gives
Those qualities upon which friendship lives.
How much it means that I say this to you—
Without these friendships—life, what *cauchemar!*"

Among the windings of the violins
30   And the ariettes
Of cracked cornets
Inside my brain a dull tom-tom begins
Absurdly hammering a prelude of its own,
Capricious monotone
35   That is at least one definite "false note."
—Let us take the air, in a tobacco trance,
Admire the monuments,
Discuss the late events,
Correct our watches by the public clocks.
40   Then sit for half an hour and drink our bocks.

II

Now that lilacs are in bloom
She has a bowl of lilacs in her room
And twists one in her fingers while she talks.
"Ah, my friend, you do not know, you do not know
45   What life is, you who hold it in your hands";
(Slowly twisting the lilac stalks)
"You let it flow from you, you let it flow,

And youth is cruel, and has no more remorse
And smiles at situations which it cannot see."
I smile, of course,
50   And go on drinking tea.
    "Yet with these April sunsets, that somehow recall
My buried life, and Paris in the Spring,
I feel immeasurably at peace, and find the world
55   To be wonderful and youthful, after all."

The voice returns like the insistent out-of-tune
Of a broken violin on an August afternoon:
"I am always sure that you understand
My feelings, always sure that you feel,
60   Sure that across the gulf you reach your hand.

You are invulnerable, you have no Achilles' heel.
You will go on, and when you have prevailed
You can say: at this point many a one has failed.
But what have I, but what have I, my friend,
65   To give you, what can you receive from me?
Only the friendship and the sympathy
Of one about to reach her journey's end.

I shall sit here, serving tea to friends. . . ."

I take my hat: how can I make a cowardly amends
70   For what she has said to me?
You will see me any morning in the park
Reading the comics and the sporting page.
Particularly I remark

An English countess goes upon the stage.
75   A Greek was murdered at a Polish dance,
     Another bank defaulter has confessed.
     I keep my countenance,
     I remain self-possessed
     Except when a street-piano, mechanical and tired
80   Reiterates some worn-out common song
     With the smell of hyacinths across the garden
     Recalling things that other people have desired.
     Are these ideas right or wrong?

                         III
        The October night comes down: returning as before
85   Except for a slight sensation of being ill at ease
     I mount the stairs and turn the handle of the door
     And feel as if I had mounted on my hands and knees.
     "And so you are going abroad; and when do you return?
     But that's a useless question.
90   You hardly know when you are coming back,
     You will find so much to learn."
     My smile falls heavily among the bric-à-brac.

     "Perhaps you can write to me."
     My self-possession flares up for a second;
95   *This* is as I had reckoned.
     "I have been wondering frequently of late
     (But our beginnings never know our ends!)
     Why we have not developed into friends."
     I feel like one who smiles, and turning shall remark
100 Suddenly, his expression in a glass.
     My self-possession gutters; we are really in the dark.

"For everybody said so, all our friends,
They all were sure our feelings would relate
So closely! I myself can hardly understand.
105   We must leave it now to fate.
You will write, at any rate.
Perhaps it is not too late.
I shall sit here, serving tea to friends."

And I must borrow every changing shape
To find expression . . . dance, dance
110   Like a dancing bear,
Cry like a parrot, chatter like an ape.
Let us take the air, in a tobacco trance—

Well! and what if she should die some afternoon,
115   Afternoon grey and smoky, evening yellow and rose;
Should die and leave me sitting pen in hand
With the smoke coming down above the housetops;
Doubtful, for quite a while
Not knowing what to feel or if I understand
Or whether wise or foolish, tardy or too soon . . .
120   Would she not have the advantage, after all?
This music is successful with a "dying fall"
Now that we talk of dying—
And should I have the right to smile?

PRELUDES

I

The winter evening settles down
With smell of steaks in passageways.
Six o'clock.
The burnt-out ends of smoky days.
5   And now a gusty shower wraps
The grimy scraps
Of withered leaves about your feet
And newspapers from vacant lots;
The showers beat
10 On broken blinds and chimney-pots,
And at the corner of the street
A lonely cab-horse steams and stamps.
And then the lighting of the lamps.

II

The morning comes to consciousness
Of faint stale smells of beer
From the sawdust-trampled street
With all its muddy feet that press
5   To early coffee-stands.
With the other masquerades
That time resumes,
One thinks of all the hands
That are raising dingy shades
10 In a thousand furnished rooms.

III

You tossed a blanket from the bed,
You lay upon your back, and waited;
You dozed, and watched the night revealing
The thousand sordid images
5   Of which your soul was constituted;
They flickered against the ceiling.
And when all the world came back
And the light crept up between the shutters,
And you heard the sparrows in the gutters,
10   You had such a vision of the street
As the street hardly understands;
Sitting along the bed's edge, where
You curled the papers from your hair,
Or clasped the yellow soles of feet
15   In the palms of both soiled hands.

IV

His soul stretched tight across the skies
That fade behind a city block,
Or trampled by insistent feet
At four and five and six o'clock;
5   And short square fingers stuffing pipes,
And evening newspapers, and eyes
Assured of certain certainties,
The conscience of a blackened street
Impatient to assume the world.
10   I am moved by fancies that are curled
Around these images, and cling:

The notion of some infinitely gentle
Infinitely suffering thing.
Wipe your hand across your mouth, and laugh;
15   The worlds revolve like ancient women
Gathering fuel in vacant lots.

RHAPSODY ON A WINDY NIGHT

Twelve o'clock.
Along the reaches of the street
Held in a lunar synthesis,
Whispering lunar incantations
5   Dissolve the floors of the memory
And all its clear relations,
Its divisions and precisions.
Every street-lamp that I pass
Beats like a fatalistic drum,
10   And through the spaces of the dark
Midnight shakes the memory
As a madman shakes a dead geranium.

Half-past one,
The street-lamp sputtered,
15   The street-lamp muttered,
The street-lamp said, "Regard that woman
Who hesitates toward you in the light of the door
Which opens on her like a grin.
You see the border of her dress
20   Is torn and stained with sand,
And you see the corner of her eye
Twists like a crooked pin."

The memory throws up high and dry
A crowd of twisted things;
25   A twisted branch upon the beach
Eaten smooth, and polished

As if the world gave up
The secret of its skeleton,
Stiff and white.
30   A broken spring in a factory yard,
Rust that clings to the form that the strength has left
Hard and curled and ready to snap.

Half-past two,
The street-lamp said,
35   "Remark the cat which flattens itself in the gutter,
Slips out its tongue
And devours a morsel of rancid butter."
So the hand of the child, automatic,
Slipped out and pocketed a toy that was running along the
        quay.
40   I could see nothing behind that child's eye.
I have seen eyes in the street
Trying to peer through lighted shutters,
And a crab one afternoon in a pool,
An old crab with barnacles on his back,
45   Gripped the end of a stick which I held him.

Half-past three,
The lamp sputtered,
The lamp muttered in the dark.
The lamp hummed:
50   "Regard the moon,
La lune ne garde aucune rancune,
She winks a feeble eye,
She smiles into corners.
She smooths the hair of the grass.

55   The moon has lost her memory.
      A washed-out smallpox cracks her face,
      Her hand twists a paper rose,
      That smells of dust and old Cologne,
      She is alone
60   With all the old nocturnal smells
      That cross and cross across her brain.
      The reminiscence comes
      Of sunless dry geraniums
      And dust in crevices,
65   Smells of chestnuts in the streets,
      And female smells in shuttered rooms,
      And cigarettes in corridors
      And cocktail smells in bars."

      The lamp said,
70   "Four o'clock,
      Here is the number on the door.
      Memory!
      You have the key,
      The little lamp spreads a ring on the stair.
75   Mount.
      The bed is open; the tooth-brush hangs on the wall,
      Put your shoes at the door, sleep, prepare for life."

      The last twist of the knife.

MORNING AT THE WINDOW

They are rattling breakfast plates in basement kitchens,
And along the trampled edges of the street
I am aware of the damp souls of housemaids
Sprouting despondently at area gates.

5 The brown waves of fog toss up to me
Twisted faces from the bottom of the street,
And tear from a passer-by with muddy skirts
An aimless smile that hovers in the air
And vanishes along the level of the roofs.

THE "BOSTON EVENING TRANSCRIPT"

The readers of the *Boston Evening Transcript*
Sway in the wind like a field of ripe corn.

When evening quickens faintly in the street,
Wakening the appetites of life in some
And to others bringing the *Boston Evening Transcript*,
I mount the steps and ring the bell, turning
Wearily, as one would turn to nod good-bye to La
  Rochefoucauld,
If the street were time and he at the end of the street,
And I say, "Cousin Harriet, here is the *Boston Evening
  Transcript*."

AUNT HELEN

Miss Helen Slingsby was my maiden aunt,
And lived in a small house near a fashionable square
Cared for by servants to the number of four.
Now when she died there was silence in heaven
5   And silence at her end of the street.
The shutters were drawn and the undertaker wiped his
    feet—
He was aware that this sort of thing had occurred before.
The dogs were handsomely provided for,
But shortly afterwards the parrot died too.
10   The Dresden clock continued ticking on the mantelpiece,
And the footman sat upon the dining-table
Holding the second housemaid on his knees—
Who had always been so careful while her mistress lived.

COUSIN NANCY

Miss Nancy Ellicott
Strode across the hills and broke them,
Rode across the hills and broke them—
The barren New England hills—
5   Riding to hounds
Over the cow-pasture.

Miss Nancy Ellicott smoked
And danced all the modern dances;
And her aunts were not quite sure how they felt about it,
10   But they knew that it was modern.

Upon the glazen shelves kept watch
Matthew and Waldo, guardians of the faith,
The army of unalterable law.

MR. APOLLINAX

Ὦ τῆς καινότητος. Ἡράκλεις, τῆς παραδοξολογίας.
εὐμήχανος ἄνθρωπος.

—Lucian

When Mr. Apollinax visited the United States
His laughter tinkled among the teacups.
I thought of Fragilion, that shy figure among the
    birch-trees,
And of Priapus in the shrubbery
5   Gaping at the lady in the swing.
In the palace of Mrs. Phlaccus, at Professor Channing-
    Cheetah's
He laughed like an irresponsible foetus.
His laughter was submarine and profound
Like the old man of the sea's
10   Hidden under coral islands
Where worried bodies of drowned men drift down in the
    green silence,
Dropping from fingers of surf.
I looked for the head of Mr. Apollinax rolling under a chair
Or grinning over a screen
15   With seaweed in its hair.
I heard the beat of centaur's hoofs over the hard turf
As his dry and passionate talk devoured the afternoon.
"He is a charming man"—"But after all what did he
    mean?"—
"His pointed ears. . . . He must be unbalanced."—

20   "There was something he said that I might have
         challenged."
      Of dowager Mrs. Phlaccus, and Professor and
         Mrs. Cheetah
      I remember a slice of lemon, and a bitten macaroon.

HYSTERIA

As she laughed I was aware of becoming involved in her laughter and being part of it, until her teeth were only accidental stars with a talent for squad-drill. I was drawn in by short gasps, inhaled at each momentary recovery, lost finally in the dark caverns of her throat, bruised by the ripple of unseen muscles. An elderly waiter with trembling hands was hurriedly spreading a pink and white checked cloth over the rusty green iron table, saying: "If the lady and gentleman wish to take their tea in the garden, if the lady and gentleman wish to take their tea in the garden . . ." I decided that if the shaking of her breasts could be stopped, some of the fragments of the afternoon might be collected, and I concentrated my attention with careful subtlety to this end.

CONVERSATION GALANTE

I observe: "Our sentimental friend the moon!
Or possibly (fantastic, I confess)
It may be Prester John's balloon
Or an old battered lantern hung aloft
5   To light poor travellers to their distress."
    She then: "How you digress!"

And I then: "Someone frames upon the keys
That exquisite nocturne, with which we explain
The night and moonshine; music which we seize
10   To body forth our own vacuity."
    She then: "Does this refer to me?"
    "Oh no, it is I who am inane."

"You, madam, are the eternal humorist,
The eternal enemy of the absolute,
15   Giving our vagrant moods the slightest twist!
With your air indifferent and imperious
At a stroke our mad poetics to confute—"
    And—"Are we then so serious?"

LA FIGLIA CHE PIANGE

O quam te memorem virgo . . .

Stand on the highest pavement of the stair—
Lean on a garden urn—
Weave, weave the sunlight in your hair—
Clasp your flowers to you with a pained surprise—
5 Fling them to the ground and turn
With a fugitive resentment in your eyes:
But weave, weave the sunlight in your hair.

So I would have had him leave,
So I would have had her stand and grieve,
10 So he would have left
As the soul leaves the body torn and bruised,
As the mind deserts the body it has used.
I should find
Some way incomparably light and deft,
15 Some way we both should understand,
Simple and faithless as a smile and shake of the hand.

She turned away, but with the autumn weather
Compelled my imagination many days,
Many days and many hours:
20 Her hair over her arms and her arms full of flowers.
And I wonder how they should have been together!
I should have lost a gesture and a pose.
Sometimes these cogitations still amaze
The troubled midnight and the noon's repose.

POEMS
1920

GERONTION

Thou hast nor youth nor age
But as it were an after dinner sleep
Dreaming of both.

Here I am, an old man in a dry month,
Being read to by a boy, waiting for rain.
I was neither at the hot gates
Nor fought in the warm rain
5   Nor knee deep in the salt marsh, heaving a cutlass,
Bitten by flies, fought.
My house is a decayed house,
And the Jew squats on the window-sill, the owner,
Spawned in some estaminet of Antwerp,
10   Blistered in Brussels, patched and peeled in London.
The goat coughs at night in the field overhead;
Rocks, moss, stonecrop, iron, merds.
The woman keeps the kitchen, makes tea,
Sneezes at evening, poking the peevish gutter.
15   I an old man,
A dull head among windy spaces.

Signs are taken for wonders. "We would see a sign!"
The word within a word, unable to speak a word,
Swaddled with darkness. In the juvescence of the year
20   Came Christ the tiger
In depraved May, dogwood and chestnut, flowering judas,
To be eaten, to be divided, to be drunk
Among whispers; by Mr. Silvero

With caressing hands, at Limoges
25 Who walked all night in the next room;
By Hakagawa, bowing among the Titians;
By Madame de Tornquist, in the dark room
Shifting the candles; Fräulein von Kulp
Who turned in the hall, one hand on the door.
    Vacant shuttles
30 Weave the wind. I have no ghosts,
An old man in a draughty house
Under a windy knob.

After such knowledge, what forgiveness? Think now
History has many cunning passages, contrived corridors
35 And issues, deceives with whispering ambitions,
Guides us by vanities. Think now
She gives when our attention is distracted
And what she gives, gives with such supple confusions
That the giving famishes the craving. Gives too late
40 What's not believed in, or if still believed,
In memory only, reconsidered passion. Gives too soon
Into weak hands, what's thought can be dispensed with
Till the refusal propagates a fear. Think
Neither fear nor courage saves us. Unnatural vices
45 Are fathered by our heroism. Virtues
Are forced upon us by our impudent crimes.
These tears are shaken from the wrath-bearing tree.

The tiger springs in the new year. Us he devours. Think at
    last
We have not reached conclusion, when I
50 Stiffen in a rented house. Think at last

I have not made this show purposelessly
And it is not by any concitation
Of the backward devils.
I would meet you upon this honestly.
55 I that was near your heart was removed therefrom
To lose beauty in terror, terror in inquisition.
I have lost my passion: why should I need to keep it
Since what is kept must be adulterated?
I have lost my sight, smell, hearing, taste and touch:
60 How should I use them for your closer contact?

These with a thousand small deliberations
Protract the profit of their chilled delirium,
Excite the membrane, when the sense has cooled,
With pungent sauces, multiply variety
65 In a wilderness of mirrors. What will the spider do,
Suspend its operations, will the weevil
Delay? De Bailhache, Fresca, Mrs. Cammel, whirled
Beyond the circuit of the shuddering Bear
In fractured atoms. Gull against the wind, in the windy
    straits
70 Of Belle Isle, or running on the Horn.
White feathers in the snow, the Gulf claims,
And an old man driven on the Trades
To a sleepy corner.

                    Tenants of the house,
75 Thoughts of a dry brain in a dry season.

BURBANK WITH A BAEDEKER:
BLEISTEIN WITH A CIGAR

Tra-la-la-la-la-la-laire—nil nisi divinum stabile est;
caetera fumus—the gondola stopped, the old palace was
there, how charming its grey and pink—goats and mon-
keys, with such hair too!—so the countess passed on until
she came through the little park, where Niobe presented
her with a cabinet, and so departed.

Burbank crossed a little bridge
    Descending at a small hotel;
Princess Volupine arrived,
    They were together, and he fell.

5 Defunctive music under sea
    Passed seaward with the passing bell
Slowly: the God Hercules
    Had left him, that had loved him well.

The horses, under the axletree
10   Beat up the dawn from Istria
With even feet. Her shuttered barge
    Burned on the water all the day.

But this or such was Bleistein's way:
    A saggy bending of the knees
15 And elbows, with the palms turned out,
    Chicago Semite Viennese.

A lustreless protrusive eye
    Stares from the protozoic slime
At a perspective of Canaletto.
20   The smoky candle end of time

Declines. On the Rialto once.
    The rats are underneath the piles.
The Jew is underneath the lot.
    Money in furs. The boatman smiles,

25   Princess Volupine extends
    A meagre, blue-nailed, phthisic hand
To climb the waterstair. Lights, lights,
    She entertains Sir Ferdinand

Klein. Who clipped the lion's wings
30   And flea'd his rump and pared his claws?
Thought Burbank, meditating on
    Time's ruins, and the seven laws.

SWEENEY ERECT

And the trees about me,
Let them be dry and leafless; let the rocks
Groan with continual surges; and behind me
Make all a desolation. Look, look, wenches!

Paint me a cavernous waste shore
    Cast in the unstilled Cyclades,
Paint me the bold anfractuous rocks
    Faced by the snarled and yelping seas.

5   Display me Aeolus above
    Reviewing the insurgent gales
Which tangle Ariadne's hair
    And swell with haste the perjured sails.

Morning stirs the feet and hands
10   (Nausicaa and Polypheme).
Gesture of orang-outang
    Rises from the sheets in steam.

This withered root of knots of hair
    Slitted below and gashed with eyes,
15 This oval O cropped out with teeth:
    The sickle motion from the thighs

Jackknifes upward at the knees
    Then straightens out from heel to hip
Pushing the framework of the bed
20   And clawing at the pillow slip.

Sweeney addressed full length to shave
    Broadbottomed, pink from nape to base,
Knows the female temperament
    And wipes the suds around his face.

25   (The lengthened shadow of a man
        Is history, said Emerson
Who had not seen the silhouette
    Of Sweeney straddled in the sun.)

Tests the razor on his leg
30   Waiting until the shriek subsides.
The epileptic on the bed
    Curves backward, clutching at her sides.

The ladies of the corridor
    Find themselves involved, disgraced,
35 Call witness to their principles
    And deprecate the lack of taste

Observing that hysteria
    Might easily be misunderstood;
Mrs. Turner intimates
40   It does the house no sort of good.

But Doris, towelled from the bath,
    Enters padding on broad feet,
Bringing sal volatile
    And a glass of brandy neat.

A COOKING EGG

En l'an trentiesme de mon aage
Que toutes mes hontes j'ay beues . . .

Pipit sate upright in her chair
    Some distance from where I was sitting;
Views of Oxford Colleges
    Lay on the table with the knitting.

5 Daguerreotypes and silhouettes,
    Her grandfather and great great aunts,
Supported on the mantelpiece
    An *Invitation to the Dance*.

                * * * *

I shall not want Honour in Heaven
10   For I shall meet Sir Philip Sidney
And have talk with Coriolanus
    And other heroes of that kidney.

I shall not want Capital in Heaven
    For I shall meet Sir Alfred Mond.
15 We two shall lie together, lapt
    In a five per cent. Exchequer Bond.

I shall not want Society in Heaven,
    Lucretia Borgia shall be my Bride;
Her anecdotes will be more amusing
20   Than Pipit's experience could provide.

I shall not want Pipit in Heaven:
    Madame Blavatsky will instruct me
In the Seven Sacred Trances;
    Piccarda de Donati will conduct me.

* * * *

25   But where is the penny world I bought
        To eat with Pipit behind the screen?
The red-eyed scavengers are creeping
        From Kentish Town and Golder's Green;

Where are the eagles and the trumpets?

30   Buried beneath some snow-deep Alps.
Over buttered scones and crumpets
    Weeping, weeping multitudes
Droop in a hundred A.B.C.'s.

LE DIRECTEUR

Malheur à la malheureuse Tamise!
Qui coule si près du Spectateur.
Le directeur
Conservateur
5 Du Spectateur
Empeste la brise.
Les actionnaires
Réactionnaires
Du Spectateur
10 Conservateur
Bras dessus bras dessous
Font des tours
A pas de loup.
Dans un égout
15 Une petite fille
En guenilles
Camarde
Regarde
Le directeur
20 Du Spectateur
Conservateur
Et crève d'amour.

MÉLANGE ADULTÈRE DE TOUT

En Amérique, professeur;
En Angleterre, journaliste;
C'est à grands pas et en sueur
Que vous suivrez à peine ma piste.
5   En Yorkshire, conférencier;
A Londres, un peu banquier,
Vous me paierez bien la tête.
C'est à Paris que je me coiffe
Casque noir de jemenfoutiste.
10   En Allemagne, philosophe
Surexcité par Emporheben
Au grand air de Bergsteigleben;
J'erre toujours de-ci de-là
A divers coups de tra là là
15   De Damas jusqu' à Omaha;
Je célébrai mon jour de fête
Dans une oasis d'Afrique
Vêtu d'une peau de girafe.

On montrera mon cénotaphe
20   Aux côtes brûlantes de Mozambique.

LUNE DE MIEL

Ils ont vu les Pay-Bas, ils rentrent à Terre Haute;
Mais une nuit d'été, les voici à Ravenne,
A l'aise entre deux draps, chez deux centaines de punaises;
La sueur aestivale, et une forte odeur de chienne.
5   Ils restent sur le dos écartant les genoux
De quatre jambes molles tout gonflées de morsures.
On relève le drap pour mieux égratigner.
Moins d'une lieue d'ici est Saint Apollinaire
En Classe, basilique connue des amateurs
10 De chapitaux d'acanthe que tournoie le vent.

Ils vont prendre le train de huit heures
Prolonger leurs misères de Padoue à Milan
Où se trouve la Cène, et un restaurant pas cher.
Lui pense aux pourboires, et rédige son bilan.
15 Ils auront vu la Suisse et traversé la France.
Et Saint Apollinaire, raide et ascétique,
Vieille usine désaffectée de Dieu, tient encore
Dans ses pierres écroulantes la forme précise de Byzance.

THE HIPPOPOTAMUS

*And when this epistle is read among you, cause that it be
read also in the church of the Laodiceans.*

The broad-backed hippopotamus
Rests on his belly in the mud;
Although he seems so firm to us
He is merely flesh and blood.

5   Flesh and blood is weak and frail,
Susceptible to nervous shock;
While the True Church can never fail
For it is based upon a rock.

The hippo's feeble steps may err
10   In compassing material ends,
While the True Church need never stir
To gather in its dividends.

The 'potamus can never reach
The mango on the mango-tree;
15   But fruits of pomegranate and peach
Refresh the Church from over sea.

At mating time the hippo's voice
Betrays inflexions hoarse and odd,
But every week we hear rejoice
20   The Church, at being one with God.

The hippopotamus's day
Is passed in sleep; at night he hunts;
God works in a mysterious way—
The Church can sleep and feed at once.

25   I saw the 'potamus take wing
Ascending from the damp savannas,
And quiring angels round him sing
The praise of God, in loud hosannas.

Blood of the Lamb shall wash him clean
30   And him shall heavenly arms enfold,
Among the saints he shall be seen
Performing on a harp of gold.

He shall be washed as white as snow,
By all the martyr'd virgins kist,
35   While the True Church remains below
Wrapt in the old miasmal mist.

DANS LE RESTAURANT

Le garçon délabré qui n'a rien à faire
Que de se gratter les doigts et se pencher sur mon épaule:
  "Dans mon pays il fera temps pluvieux,
  Du vent, du grand soleil, et de la pluie;
5 C'est ce qu'on appelle le jour de lessive des gueux."
(Bavard, baveux, à la croupe arrondie,
Je te prie, au moins, ne bave pas dans la soupe).
  "Les saules trempés, et des bourgeons sur les ronces—
  C'est là, dans une averse, qu'on s'abrite.
10 J'avais sept ans, elle était plus petite.
  Ellé était toute mouillée, je lui ai donné des primevères."
Les taches de son gilet montent au chiffre de trente-huit.
  "Je la chatouillais, pour la fair rire.
  Elle avait une odeur fraîche, qui m'était inconnue."
15 Mais alors, vieux lubrique, à cet âge . . .
"Monsieur, le fait est dur.
  Il est venu, nous peloter, un gros chien;
  Moi j'avais peur, je l'ai quittée à mi-chemin.
  C'est dommage."
20   Mais alors, tu as ton vautour!
Va t'en te décrotter les rides du visage;
Tiens, ma fourchette, décrasse-toi le crâne.
De quel droit payes-tu des expériences comme moi?
Tiens, voilà dix sous, pour la salle-de-bains.

25 Phlébas, le Phénicien, pendant quinze jours noyé,
Oubliait les cris des mouettes et la houle de Cornouaille,

Et les profits et les pertes, et la cargaison d'étain:
Un courant de sous-mer l'emporta trés loin,
Le repassant aux étapes de sa vie antérieure.
30   Figurez-vous donc, c'était un sort pénible;
Cependant, ce fut jadis un bel homme, de haute taille.

WHISPERS OF IMMORTALITY

Webster was much possessed by death
And saw the skull beneath the skin;
And breastless creatures under ground
Leaned backward with a lipless grin.

5   Daffodil bulbs instead of balls
Stared from the sockets of the eyes!
He knew that thought clings round dead limbs
Tightening its lusts and luxuries.

Donne, I suppose, was such another
10   Who found no substitute for sense,
To seize and clutch and penetrate;
Expert beyond experience,

He knew the anguish of the marrow
The ague of the skeleton;
15   No contact possible to flesh
Allayed the fever of the bone.

                  * * * *

Grishkin is nice: her Russian eye
Is underlined for emphasis;
Uncorseted, her friendly bust
20   Gives promise of pneumatic bliss.

The couched Brazilian jaguar
Compels the scampering marmoset

With subtle effluence of cat;
Grishkin has a maisonnette;

25   The sleek Brazilian jaguar
Does not in its arboreal gloom
Distil so rank a feline smell
As Grishkin in a drawing-room.

And even the Abstract Entities
30   Circumambulate her charm;
But our lot crawls between dry ribs
To keep our metaphysics warm.

MR. ELIOT'S SUNDAY MORNING SERVICE

Look, look, master, here comes two religious caterpillars.
—The Jew of Malta

Polyphiloprogenitive
The sapient sutlers of the Lord
Drift across the window-panes.
In the beginning was the Word.

5   In the beginning was the Word.
Superfetation of τό ἕν,
And at the mensual turn of time
Produced enervate Origen.

A painter of the Umbrian school
10 Designed upon a gesso ground
The nimbus of the Baptized God.
The wilderness is cracked and browned.

But through the water pale and thin
Still shine the unoffending feet
15 And there above the painter set
The Father and the Paraclete.

* * * *

The sable presbyters approach
The avenue of penitence;
The young are red and pustular
20 Clutching piaculative pence.

Under the penitential gates
Sustained by staring Seraphim
Where the souls of the devout
Burn invisible and dim.

25 Along the garden-wall the bees
With hairy bellies pass between
The staminate and pistillate,
Blest office of the epicene.

Sweeney shifts from ham to ham
30 Stirring the water in his bath.
The masters of the subtle schools
Are controversial, polymath.

SWEENEY AMONG THE NIGHTINGALES

ὤμοι, πέπληγμαι καιρίαν πληγὴν ἔσω.
Apeneck Sweeney spreads his knees
Letting his arms hang down to laugh,
The zebra stripes along his jaw
Swelling to maculate giraffe.

5 The circles of the stormy moon
Slide westward toward the River Plate,
Death and the Raven drift above
And Sweeney guards the hornèd gate.

Gloomy Orion and the Dog
10 Are veiled; and hushed the shrunken seas;
The person in the Spanish cape
Tries to sit on Sweeney's knees

Slips and pulls the table cloth
Overturns a coffee-cup,
15 Reorganized upon the floor
She yawns and draws a stocking up;

The silent man in mocha brown
Sprawls at the window-sill and gapes;
The waiter brings in oranges
20 Bananas figs and hothouse grapes;

The silent vertebrate exhales,
Contracts and concentrates, withdraws;

Rachel *née* Rabinovitch
Tears at the grapes with murderous paws;

25   She and the lady in the cape
Are suspect, thought to be in league;
Therefore the man with heavy eyes
Declines the gambit, shows fatigue,

Leaves the room and reappears
30   Outside the window, leaning in,
Branches of wistaria
Circumscribe a golden grin;

The host with someone indistinct
Converses at the door apart,
35   The nightingales are singing near
The Convent of the Sacred Heart,

And sang within the bloody wood
When Agamemnon cried aloud
And let their liquid siftings fall
40   To stain the stiff dishonoured shroud.

THE WASTE LAND
1922

*"Nam Sibyllam quidem Cumis ego ipse oculis meis
vidi in ampulla pendere, et cum illi pueri dicerent:
Σίβνλλα τί θέλεις; respondebat illa: ἀποθανεῖν θέλω."*

For Ezra Pound
il miglior fabbro.

I. The Burial of the Dead

April is the cruellest month, breeding
Lilacs out of the dead land, mixing
Memory and desire, stirring
Dull roots with spring rain.
5   Winter kept us warm, covering
Earth in forgetful snow, feeding
A little life with dried tubers.
Summer surprised us, coming over the Starnbergersee
With a shower of rain; we stopped in the colonnade,
10 And went on in sunlight, into the Hofgarten,
And drank coffee, and talked for an hour.
Bin gar keine Russin, stamm' aus Litauen, echt deutsch.
And when we were children, staying at the arch-duke's,
My cousin's, he took me out on a sled,
15 And I was frightened. He said, Marie,
Marie, hold on tight. And down we went.
In the mountains, there you feel free.
I read, much of the night, and go south in the winter.

What are the roots that clutch, what branches grow
20 Out of this stony rubbish? Son of man,
You cannot say, or guess, for you know only
A heap of broken images, where the sun beats,
And the dead tree gives no shelter, the cricket no relief,
And the dry stone no sound of water. Only
25 There is shadow under this red rock,
(Come in under the shadow of this red rock),
And I will show you something different from either
Your shadow at morning striding behind you

Or your shadow at evening rising to meet you;
30   I will show you fear in a handful of dust.

      Frisch weht der Wind
      Der Heimat zu
      Mein Irisch Kind,
      Wo weilest du?

35   "You gave me Hyacinths first a year ago;
      "They called me the hyacinth girl."
      —Yet when we came back, late, from the hyacinth garden,
      Your arms full, and your hair wet, I could not
      Speak, and my eyes failed, I was neither
40   Living nor dead, and I knew nothing,
      Looking into the heart of light, the silence.
      Oed' und leer das Meer.

      Madame Sosostris, famous clairvoyante,
      Had a bad cold, nevertheless
45   Is known to be the wisest woman in Europe,
      With a wicked pack of cards. Here, said she,
      Is your card, the drowned Phoenician Sailor,
      (Those are pearls that were his eyes. Look!)
      Here is Belladonna, the Lady of the Rocks,
50   The lady of situations.
      Here is the man with three staves, and here the Wheel,
      And here is the one-eyed merchant, and this card,
      Which is blank, is something he carries on his back,
      Which I am forbidden to see. I do not find
55   The Hanged Man. Fear death by water.
      I see crowds of people, walking round in a ring.

Thank you. If you see dear Mrs. Equitone,
Tell her I bring the horoscope myself:
One must be so careful these days.

60   Unreal City,
     Under the brown fog of a winter dawn,
     A crowd flowed over London Bridge, so many,
     I had not thought death had undone so many.
     Sighs, short and infrequent, were exhaled,
65   And each man fixed his eyes before his feet.
     Flowed up the hill and down King William Street,
     To where Saint Mary Woolnoth kept the hours
     With a dead sound on the final stroke of nine.
     There I saw one I knew, and stopped him, crying: "Stetson!
70   "You who were with me in the ships at Mylae!
     "That corpse you planted last year in your garden,
     "Has it begun to sprout? Will it bloom this year?
     "Or has the sudden frost disturbed its bed?
     "O keep the Dog far hence, that's friend to men,
75   "Or with his nails he'll dig it up again!
     "You! hypocrite lecteur!—mon semblable,—mon frère!"

                    II. A Game of Chess
          The Chair she sat in, like a burnished throne,
     Glowed on the marble, where the glass
     Held up by standards wrought with fruited vines
80   From which a golden Cupidon peeped out
     (Another hid his eyes behind his wing)
     Doubled the flames of sevenbranched candelabra
     Reflecting light upon the table as
     The glitter of her jewels rose to meet it,

85   From satin cases poured in rich profusion.
      In vials of ivory and coloured glass
      Unstoppered, lurked her strange synthetic perfumes,
      Unguent, powdered, or liquid—troubled, confused
      And drowned the sense in odours; stirred by the air
90   That freshened from the window, these ascended
      In fattening the prolonged candle-flames,
      Flung their smoke into the laquearia,
      Stirring the pattern on the coffered ceiling.
      Huge sea-wood fed with copper
95   Burned green and orange, framed by the coloured stone,
      In which sad light a carvèd dolphin swam.
      Above the antique mantel was displayed
      As though a window gave upon the sylvan scene
      The change of Philomel, by the barbarous king
100   So rudely forced; yet there the nightingale
      Filled all the desert with inviolable voice
      And still she cried, and still the world pursues,
      "Jug Jug" to dirty ears.
      And other withered stumps of time
105   Were told upon the walls; staring forms
      Leaned out, leaning, hushing the room enclosed.
      Footsteps shuffled on the stair.
      Under the firelight, under the brush, her hair
      Spread out in fiery points
110   Glowed into words, then would be savagely still.

      "My nerves are bad to-night. Yes, bad. Stay with me.
      Speak to me. Why do you never speak? Speak.
           What are you thinking of? What thinking? What?
      I never know what you are thinking. Think."

115 I think we are in rats' alley
 Where the dead men lost their bones.

  "What is that noise?"
         The wind under the door.
  "What is that noise now? What is the wind doing?"
120   Nothing again nothing.
               "Do
 You know nothing? Do you see nothing? Do you
  remember
 "Nothing?"

 I remember
125 Those are pearls that were his eyes.
 "Are you alive, or not? Is there nothing in your head?"
              But

 O O O O that Shakespeherian Rag—
 It's so elegant
130 So intelligent
 "What shall I do now? What shall I do?
 I shall rush out as I am, and walk the street
 With my hair down, so. What shall we do tomorrow?
 What shall we ever do?"
135   The hot water at ten.
 And if it rains, a closed car at four.
 And we shall play a game of chess,
 Pressing lidless eyes and waiting for a knock upon the door.

  When Lil's husband got demobbed, I said—
140 I didn't mince my words, I said to her myself,
 Hurry up please its time

Now Albert's coming back, make yourself a bit smart.
He'll want to know what you done with that money he
    gave you
To get yourself some teeth. He did, I was there.
145   You have them all out, Lil, and get a nice set,
He said, I swear, I can't bear to look at you.
And no more can't I, I said, and think of poor Albert,
He's been in the army four years, he wants a good time,
And if you don't give it him, there's others will, I said.
150   Oh is there, she said. Something o' that, I said.
Then I'll know who to thank, she said, and give me a
    straight look.
Hurry up please its time
If you don't like it you can get on with it, I said.
Others can pick and choose if you can't.
155   But if Albert makes off, it won't be for lack of telling.
You ought to be ashamed, I said, to look so antique.
(And her only thirty-one.)
I can't help it, she said, pulling a long face,
It's them pills I took, to bring it off, she said.
160   (She's had five already, and nearly died of young George.)
The chemist said it would be all right, but I've never been
    the same.
You *are* a proper fool, I said.
Well, if Albert won't leave you alone, there it is, I said,
What you get married for if you don't want children?
165   Hurry up please its time
Well, that Sunday Albert was home, they had a hot
    gammon,
And they asked me in to dinner, to get the beauty of
    it hot—

HURRY UP PLEASE ITS TIME
HURRY UP PLEASE ITS TIME
170   Goonight Bill. Goonight Lou. Goonight May. Goonight.
Ta ta. Goonight. Goonight.
Good night, ladies, good night, sweet ladies, good night,
    good night.

III. The Fire Sermon

The river's tent is broken; the last fingers of leaf
Clutch and sink into the wet bank. The wind
175   Crosses the brown land, unheard. The nymphs are
    departed.
Sweet Thames, run softly, till I end my song.
The river bears no empty bottles, sandwich papers,
Silk handkerchiefs, cardboard boxes, cigarette ends
Or other testimony of summer nights. The nymphs are
    departed.
180   And their friends, the loitering heirs of City directors;
Departed, have left no addresses.
By the waters of Leman I sat down and wept . . .
Sweet Thames, run softly till I end my song,
Sweet Thames, run softly, for I speak not loud or long.
185   But at my back in a cold blast I hear
The rattle of the bones, and chuckle spread from ear to ear.

A rat crept softly through the vegetation
Dragging its slimy belly on the bank
While I was fishing in the dull canal
190   On a winter evening round behind the gashouse
Musing upon the king my brother's wreck
And on the king my father's death before him.

White bodies naked on the low damp ground
And bones cast in a little low dry garret,
195   Rattled by the rat's foot only, year to year.
But at my back from time to time I hear
The sound of horns and motors, which shall bring
Sweeney to Mrs. Porter in the spring.
O the moon shone bright on Mrs. Porter
200   And on her daughter
They wash their feet in soda water
Et O ces voix d'enfants, chantant dans la coupole!

Twit twit twit
Jug jug jug jug jug jug
205   So rudely forc'd.
Tereu

Unreal City
Under the brown fog of a winter noon
Mr. Eugenides, the Smyrna merchant
210   Unshaven, with a pocket full of currants
C.i.f. London: documents at sight,
Asked me in demotic French
To luncheon at the Cannon Street Hotel
Followed by a weekend at the Metropole.

215   At the violet hour, when the eyes and back
Turn upward from the desk, when the human engine waits
Like a taxi throbbing waiting,
I Tiresias, though blind, throbbing between two lives,
Old man with wrinkled female breasts, can see
220   At the violet hour, the evening hour that strives

Homeward, and brings the sailor home from sea,
The typist home at teatime, clears her breakfast, lights
Her stove, and lays out food in tins.
Out of the window perilously spread
225   Her drying combinations touched by the sun's last rays,
On the divan are piled (at night her bed)
Stockings, slippers, camisoles, and stays.
I Tiresias, old man with wrinkled dugs
Perceived the scene, and foretold the rest—
230   I too awaited the expected guest.
He, the young man carbuncular, arrives,
A small house agent's clerk, with one bold stare,
One of the low on whom assurance sits
As a silk hat on a Bradford millionaire.
235   The time is now propitious, as he guesses,
The meal is ended, she is bored and tired,
Endeavours to engage her in caresses
Which still are unreproved, if undesired.
Flushed and decided, he assaults at once;
240   Exploring hands encounter no defence;
His vanity requires no response,
And makes a welcome of indifference.
(And I Tiresias have foresuffered all
Enacted on this same divan or bed;
245   I who have sat by Thebes below the wall
And walked among the lowest of the dead.)
Bestows one final patronising kiss,
And gropes his way, finding the stairs unlit . . .

She turns and looks a moment in the glass,
250   Hardly aware of her departed lover;

Her brain allows one half-formed thought to
    pass:
"Well now that's done: and I'm glad it's over."
When lovely woman stoops to folly and
Paces about her room again, alone,
255   She smooths her hair with automatic hand,
And puts a record on the gramophone.

"This music crept by me upon the waters"
And along the Strand, up Queen Victoria Street.
O City city, I can sometimes hear
260   Beside a public bar in Lower Thames Street,
The pleasant whining of a mandoline
And a clatter and a chatter from within
Where fishmen lounge at noon: where the walls
Of Magnus Martyr hold
265   Inexplicable splendour of Ionian white and gold.

     The river sweats
     Oil and tar
     The barges drift
     With the turning tide
270   Red sails
     Wide
     To leeward, swing on the heavy spar.
     The barges wash
     Drifting logs
275   Down Greenwich reach
     Past the Isle of Dogs.
           Weialala leia
           Wallala leialala

Elizabeth and Leicester
280 Beating oars
The stern was formed
A gilded shell
Red and gold
The brisk swell
285 Rippled both shores
Southwest wind
Carried down stream
The peal of bells
White towers
290 Weialala leia
Wallala leialala

"Trams and dusty trees.
Highbury bore me. Richmond and Kew
Undid me. By Richmond I raised my knees
295 Supine on the floor of a narrow canoe."

"My feet are at Moorgate, and my heart
Under my feet. After the event
He wept. He promised 'a new start.'
I made no comment. What should I resent?"

300 "On Margate Sands.
I can connect
Nothing with nothing.
The broken fingernails of dirty hands.
My people humble people who expect
305 Nothing."
      la la

To Carthage then I came

Burning burning burning burning
O Lord Thou pluckest me out
310   O Lord Thou pluckest

burning

IV. Death by Water
Phlebas the Phoenician, a fortnight dead,
Forgot the cry of gulls, and the deep sea swell
And the profit and loss.
315   A current under sea
Picked his bones in whispers. As he rose and fell
He passed the stages of his age and youth
Entering the whirlpool.
                              Gentile or Jew
320   O you who turn the wheel and look to windward,
Consider Phlebas, who was once handsome and tall
    as you.

V. What the Thunder Said
After the torchlight red on sweaty faces
After the frosty silence in the gardens
After the agony in stony places
325   The shouting and the crying
Prison and palace and reverberation
Of thunder of spring over distant mountains
He who was living is now dead

We who were living are now dying
330   With a little patience

Here is no water but only rock
Rock and no water and the sandy road
The road winding above among the mountains
Which are mountains of rock without water
335   If there were only water amongst the rock
Amongst the rock one cannot stop or think
Sweat is dry and feet are in the sand
If there were only water amongst the rock
Dead mountain mouth of carious teeth that cannot spit
340   Here one can neither stand nor lie nor sit
There is not even silence in the mountains
But dry sterile thunder without rain
There is not even solitude in the mountains
But red sullen faces sneer and snarl
345   From doors of mudcracked houses
                              If there were water
      And no rock
      If there were rock
      And also water
350   And water
      A spring
      A pool among the rock
      If there were the sound of water only
      Not the cicada
355   And dry grass singing
      But sound of water over a rock
      Where the hermit-thrush sings in the pine trees

Drip drop drip drop drop drop drop
But there is no water

360   Who is the third who walks always beside you?
When I count, there are only you and I together
But when I look ahead up the white road
There is always another one walking beside you
Gliding wrapt in a brown mantle, hooded
365   I do not know whether a man or a woman
—But who is that on the other side of you?

What is that sound high in the air
Murmur of maternal lamentation
Who are those hooded hordes swarming
370   Over endless plains, stumbling in cracked earth
Ringed by the flat horizon only
What is the city over the mountains
Cracks and reforms and bursts in the violet air
Falling towers
375   Jerusalem Athens Alexandria
Vienna London
Unreal

A woman drew her long black hair out tight
And fiddled whisper music on those strings
And bats with baby faces in the violet light
380   Whistled, and beat their wings
And crawled head downward down a blackened wall
And upside down in air were towers
Tolling reminiscent bells, that kept the hours
And voices singing out of empty cisterns and exhausted
wells.

385 In this decayed hole among the mountains
     In the faint moonlight, the grass is singing
     Over the tumbled graves, about the chapel
     There is the empty chapel, only the wind's home.
     It has no windows, and the door swings,
390 Dry bones can harm no one.
     Only a cock stood on the rooftree
     Co co rico co co rico
     In a flash of lightning. Then a damp gust
     Bringing rain

395 Ganga was sunken, and the limp leaves
     Waited for rain, while the black clouds
     Gathered far distant, over Himavant.
     The jungle crouched, humped in silence.
     Then spoke the thunder
400 Da
     Datta: what have we given?
     My friend, blood shaking my heart
     The awful daring of a moment's surrender
     Which an age of prudence can never retract
405 By this, and this only, we have existed
     Which is not to be found in our obituaries
     Or in memories draped by the beneficent spider
     Or under seals broken by the lean solicitor
     In our empty rooms
410 Da
     Dayadhvam: I have heard the key
     Turn in the door once and turn once only
     We think of the key, each in his prison
     Thinking of the key, each confirms a prison

415   Only at nightfall, aethereal rumours
       Revive for a moment a broken Coriolanus
       DA
       Damyata: The boat responded
       Gaily, to the hand expert with sail and oar
420   The sea was calm, your heart would have responded
       Gaily, when invited, beating obedient
       To controlling hands

                              I sat upon the shore
       Fishing, with the arid plain behind me
425   Shall I at least set my lands in order?
       London Bridge is falling down falling down falling down
       Poi s'ascose nel foco che gli affina
       Quando fiam ceu chelidon—O swallow swallow
       Le Prince d'Aquitaine à la tour abolie
430   These fragments I have shored against my ruins
       Why then Ile fit you. Hieronymo's mad againe.
       Datta. Dayadhvam. Damyata.
                      Shantih shantih shantih

NOTES ON *THE WASTE LAND*

Not only the title, but the plan and a good deal of the incidental symbolism of the poem were suggested by Miss Jessie L. Weston's book on the Grail legend: *From Ritual to Romance* (Cambridge). Indeed, so deeply am I indebted, Miss Weston's book will elucidate the difficulties of the poem much better than my notes can do; and I recommend it (apart from the great interest of the book itself) to any who think such elucidation of the poem worth the trouble. To another work of anthropology I am indebted in general, one which has influenced our generation profoundly; I mean *The Golden Bough*; I have used especially the two volumes *Adonis, Attis, Osiris*. Anyone who is acquainted with these works will immediately recognise in the poem certain references to vegetation ceremonies.

I. THE BURIAL OF THE DEAD

Line 20. Cf. Ezekiel II, i.

23. Cf. Ecclesiastes XII, v.

31. V. Tristan und Isolde, I, verses 5–8.

42. Id. III, verse 24.

46. I am not familiar with the exact constitution of the Tarot pack of cards, from which I have obviously departed to suit my own convenience. The Hanged Man, a member of the traditional pack, fits my purpose in two ways: because he is associated in my mind with the Hanged God of Frazer, and because I associate him with the hooded figure in the passage of the disciples to Emmaus in Part V. The Phoenician Sailor and the Merchant appear later; also the "crowds of people," and Death by Water is executed in

Part IV. The Man with Three Staves (an authentic member of the Tarot pack) I associate, quite arbitrarily, with the Fisher King himself.

60. Cf. Baudelaire:
"Fourmillante cité, cité pleine de rêves,
"Ou le spectre en plein jour raccroche le passant."

63. Cf. Inferno III, 55–57:

> si lunga tratta
> di gente, ch'io non avrei creduto
> che morte tanta n'avesse disfatta.

64. Cf. Inferno IV, 25–27:

> Quivi, secondo che per ascoltare,
> non avea piante mai che di sospiri
> che l'aura eterna facevan tremare.

68. A phenomenon which I have often noticed.

74. Cf. the Dirge in Webster's *White Devil.*

76. V. Baudelaire, Preface to *Fleurs du Mal.*

II. A GAME OF CHESS

77. Cf. *Antony and Cleopatra*, II, ii, l. 190.

92. Laquearia. V. *Aeneid*, I, 726:
dependent lychni laquearibus aureis
incensi, et noctem flammis funalia vincunt.

98. Sylvan scene. V. Milton, *Paradise Lost*, IV, 140.

99. V. Ovid, *Metamorphoses*, VI, Philomela.

100. Cf. Part III, l. 204.

115. Cf. Part III, l. 195.

118. Cf. Webster: "Is the wind in that door still?"

126. Cf. Part I, l. 37, 48.

138. Cf. the game of chess in Middleton's *Women beware Women.*

III. THE FIRE SERMON

176. V. Spenser, *Prothalamion.*

192. Cf. *The Tempest*, I, ii.

196. Cf. Marvell, *To His Coy Mistress.*

197. Cf. Day, *Parliament of Bees*:

> "When of the sudden, listening, you shall hear,
> "A noise of horns and hunting, which shall bring
> "Actaeon to Diana in the spring,
> "Where all shall see her naked skin . . ."

199. I do not know the origin of the ballad from which these lines are taken: it was reported to me from Sydney, Australia.

202. V. Verlaine, *Parsifal.*

210. The currants were quoted at a price "cost insurance and freight to London"; and the Bill of Lading, etc., were to be handed to the buyer upon payment of the sight draft.

218. Tiresias, although a mere spectator and not indeed a "character," is yet the most important personage in the poem, uniting all the rest. Just as the one-eyed merchant seller of currants, melts into the Phoenician Sailor, and the latter is not wholly distinct from Ferdinand Prince of Naples, so all the women are one woman, and the two sexes meet in Tiresias. What Tiresias *sees*, in fact, is the substance of the poem. The whole passage from Ovid is of great anthropological interest:

> . . . Cum Iunone iocos et "maior vestra profecto est
> Quam quae contingit maribus," dixisse, "voluptas."
> Illa negat; placuit quae sit sententia docti
> Quaerere Tiresiae: venus huic erat utraque nota.
> Nam duo magnorum viridi coeuntia silva
> Corpora serpentum baculi violaverat ictu
> Deque viro factus, mirabile, femina septem
> Egerat autumnos; octavo rursus eosdem

Vidit et "est vestrae si tanta potentia plagae,"
Dixit "ut auctoris sortem in contraria mutet,
Nunc quoque vos feriam!" percussis anguibus isdem
Forma prior rediit genetivaque venit imago.
Arbiter hic igitur sumptus de lite iocosa
Dicta Iovis firmat; gravius Saturnia iusto
Nec pro materia fertur doluisse suique
ludicis aeterna damnavit lumina nocte,
At pater omnipotens (neque enim licet inrita cuiquam
Facta dei fecisse deo) pro lumine adempto
Scire futura dedit poenamque levavit honore.

221. This may not appear as exact as Sappho's lines, but I had in mind the "longshore" or "dory" fisherman, who returns at nightfall.

253. V. Goldsmith, the song in *The Vicar of Wakefield*.

257. V. *The Tempest*, as above.

264. The interior of St. Magnus Martyr is to my mind one of the finest among Wren's interiors. See *The Proposed Demolition of Nineteen City Churches* (P. S. King & Son, Ltd.).

266. The Song of the (three) Thames-daughters begins here. From line 292 to 306 inclusive they speak in turn. V. *Götterdämmerung*, III, i: the Rhine-daughters.

279. V. Froude, *Elizabeth*, Vol. I, ch. iv, letter of De Quadra to Philip of Spain:

"In the afternoon we were in a barge, watching the games on the river. (The Queen) was alone with Lord Robert and myself on the poop, when they began to talk nonsense, and went so far that Lord Robert at last said, as I was on the spot there was no reason why they should not be married if the queen pleased."

293. Cf. *Purgatorio*, V. 133:

        "Ricorditi di me, che son la Pia;
        "Siena mi fe', disfecemi Maremma."

307. V. St. Augustine's *Confessions*: "to Carthage then I came, where a cauldron of unholy loves sang all about mine ears."

308. The complete text of the Buddha's Fire Sermon (which corresponds in importance to the Sermon on the Mount) from which these words are taken, will be found translated in the late Henry Clarke Warren's *Buddhism in Translation* (Harvard Oriental Series). Mr. Warren was one of the great pioneers of Buddhist studies in the Occident.

309. From St. Augustine's *Confessions* again. The collocation of these two representatives of eastern and western asceticism, as the culmination of this part of the poem, is not an accident.

V. WHAT THE THUNDER SAID

In the first part of Part V three themes are employed: the journey to Emmaus, the approach to the Chapel Perilous (see Miss Weston's book) and the present decay of eastern Europe.

357. This is *Turdus aonalaschkae pallasii*, the hermit-thrush which I have heard in Quebec Province. Chapman says (*Handbook of Birds of Eastern North America*) "it is most at home in secluded woodland and thickety retreats. . . . Its notes are not remarkable for variety or volume, but in purity and sweetness of tone and exquisite modulation they are unequalled." Its "waterdripping song" is justly celebrated.

360. The following lines were stimulated by the account of one of the Antarctic expeditions (I forget which, but I think one of Shackleton's): it was related that the party of explorers, at the extremity of their strength, had the constant delusion that there was *one more member* than could actually be counted.

366–76. Cf. Hermann Hesse, *Blick ins Chaos*: "Schon ist halb Europa, schon ist zumindest der halbe Osten Europas auf dem Wege zum Chaos, fährt betrunken im heiligen Wahn am Abgrund entlang und singt dazu, singt betrunken und hymnisch wie Dmitri Karamasoff sang. Ueber diese Lieder lacht der Bürger beleidigt, der Heilige und Seher hört sie mit Tränen."

401. "Datta, dayadhvam, damyata" (Give, sympathise, control). The fable of the meaning of the Thunder is found in the *Brihadaranyaka—Upanishad*, 5, I. A translation is found in Deussen's *Sechzig Upanishads des Veda*, p. 489.

407. Cf. Webster, *The White Devil*, V, vi:

". . . they'll remarry
Ere the worm pierce your winding-sheet, ere the spider
Make a thin curtain for your epitaphs."

411. Cf. *Inferno*, XXXIII, 46:

"ed io senti chiavar l'uscio di sotto
all' orribile torre."

Also F. H. Bradley, *Appearance and Reality*, p. 306.
"My external sensations are no less private to my self than are my thoughts or my feelings. In either case my experience falls within my own circle, a circle closed on the outside; and, with all its elements alike, every sphere is opaque to the others which surround it. . . . In brief, regarded as an existence which appears in a soul, the whole world for each is peculiar and private to that soul."

424. V. Weston: *From Ritual to Romance*; chapter on the Fisher King.

427. V. *Purgatorio*, XXVI, 148.

"'Ara vos prec per aquella valor
'que vos condus al som de l'escalina,
'sovenha vos a temps de ma dolor.'
Poi s'ascose nel foco che gli affina."

428. V. *Pervigilium Veneris*. Cf. Philomela in Parts II and III.

429. V. Gerard de Nerval, Sonnet *El Desdichado.*

431. V. Kyd's *Spanish Tragedy.*

433. Shantih. Repeated as here, a formal ending to an Upani-shad. "The Peace which passeth understanding" is our equivalent to this word.

THE HOLLOW MEN
1925

Mistah Kurtz—he dead.
 A penny for the Old Guy

I

We are the hollow men
We are the stuffed men
Leaning together
Headpiece filled with straw. Alas!
Our dried voices, when
We whisper together
Are quiet and meaningless
As wind in dry grass
Or rats' feet over broken glass
In our dry cellar

Shape without form, shade without colour,
Paralysed force, gesture without motion;

Those who have crossed
With direct eyes, to death's other Kingom
Remember us—if at all—not as lost
Violent souls, but only
As the hollow men
The stuffed men.

II

Eyes I dare not meet in dreams
In death's dream kingdom
These do not appear:
There, the eyes are
Sunlight on a broken column
There, is a tree swinging
And voices are
In the wind's singing
More distant and more solemn
Than a fading star.

Let me be no nearer
In death's dream kingdom
Let me also wear
Such deliberate disguises
Rat's coat, crowskin, crossed staves
In a field
Behaving as the wind behaves
No nearer—

Not that final meeting
In the twilight kingdom

III

This is the dead land
This is cactus land
Here the stone images
Are raised, here they receive

The supplications of a dead man's hand
Under the twinkle of a fading star.

    Is it like this
In death's other kingdom
Waking alone
At the hour when we are
Trembling with tenderness
Lips that would kiss
Form prayers to broken stone.

IV

The eyes are not here
There are no eyes here
In this valley of dying stars
In this hollow valley
This broken jaw of our lost kingdoms

    In this last of meeting places
We grope together
And avoid speech
Gathered on this beach of the tumid river

    Sightless, unless
The eyes reappear
As the perpetual star
Multifoliate rose
Of death's twilight kingdom
The hope only
Of empty men.

V

Here we go round the prickly pear
Prickly pear prickly pear
Here we go round the prickly pear
At five o'clock in the morning.

  Between the idea
And the reality
Between the motion
And the act
Falls the Shadow

                                        For Thine is the Kingdom

  Between the conception
And the creation
Between the emotion
And the response
Falls the Shadow

                                        Life is very long

    Between the desire
And the spasm
Between the potency
And the existence
Between the essence
And the descent
Falls the Shadow

For Thine is the Kingdom

　　For Thine is
Life is
For Thine is the

　　This is the way the world ends
This is the way the world ends
This is the way the world ends
Not with a bang but a whimper.